The 2003 Commemorative
Stamp Yearbook

United States Postal Service

Other books available from the United States Postal Service:

THE 2002 COMMEMORATIVE STAMP YEARBOOK

THE POSTAL SERVICE GUIDE TO U.S. STAMPS
Thirtieth Edition

The 2003 Commemorative
Stamp Yearbook

United States Postal Service

UNITED STATES
POSTAL SERVICE®

HarperResource
An Imprint of HarperCollinsPublishers

HarperCollins books may be purchased for educational, business, or sales promotional use.
For information please write: Special Markets Department, HarperCollins Publishers Inc.,
10 East 53rd Street, New York, NY 10022.

Library of Congress Cataloging-in-Publication Data has been applied for.
ISBN: 0-06-019899-0

Contents

Introduction 7

Lunar New Year: Year of the Ram 8

Black Heritage: Thurgood Marshall 10

Love 12

American Filmmaking: Behind the Scenes 14

Ohio Statehood 18

Pelican Island National Wildlife Refuge 20

Cesar E. Chavez 22

Zora Neale Hurston 24

First Flight 26

Louisiana Purchase 30

American Treasures: Mary Cassatt 32

Southeastern Lighthouses 34

Korean War Veterans Memorial 38

Old Glory 40

Nature of America: Arctic Tundra 44

District of Columbia 46

Legends of Hollywood: Audrey Hepburn 48

Early Football Heroes 50

Roy Acuff 54

Reptiles and Amphibians 56

Holiday Music Makers 60

Photo Credits 62

Acknowledgments 64

Introduction

Behind the Scenes: The 2003 Commemorative Stamp Program

WHEN I JOINED the Citizens' Stamp Advisory Committee, I had no idea what a rewarding experience was in store for me. In 1990, my second year as president of the Academy of Motion Picture Arts and Sciences, the Postal Service issued four Classic Films stamps at the Academy's theater in Hollywood. After the ceremony, the Postmaster General asked me to serve on the committee. Naturally, I jumped at the chance.

What I've discovered during my time with CSAC is that helping to choose stamp subjects is a great and humbling responsibility. Our stamps speak volumes about who we are as Americans, and they are seen, enjoyed, and passionately discussed by millions of people. With that in mind, I've tried my best to represent the interests of the public, because it's important that our stamps showcase the best our country has to offer.

I usually try not to play favorites, but this year I can't hide my enthusiasm for ten stamps that are very special to me. I am truly pleased to see three years of hard work come to fruition with the American Filmmaking stamps. The Postal Service has done a wonderful job of honoring so many great actors since the Legends of Hollywood series began in 1995, and now the people behind the scenes are finally receiving recognition as well. You see their names in the credits after every movie, but these new stamps show you just how crucial these talented individuals are to the art of filmmaking. With the Academy celebrating its 75th anniversary this year, it's the perfect time to celebrate their accomplishments.

For 13 years, I've been lucky to know another talented cast of creative professionals who work behind the scenes: the designers, art directors, artists, photographers, and consultants who create our nation's stamps. In this new edition of the Commemorative Stamp Yearbook, they offer their thoughts on this challenging task, and their comments and perspectives are a real treat to read. When you see how much thought and research goes into each new stamp, you will no doubt be as impressed as I have been.

One of the best parts of serving as a CSAC member is being able to see what the Postal Service is considering for future years. I'm proud to say that upcoming stamps will continue the fine tradition of honoring the people, institutions, and historic events that make America great. So keep your eye on the stamp program. The best is yet to come.

Karl Malden

FACING PAGE: *Karl Malden and director John Frankenheimer behind the scenes during the filming of* Bird Man of Alcatraz. ABOVE LEFT: *Malden with Vivien Leigh in* A Streetcar Named Desire. ABOVE RIGHT: *As an actor for more than five decades, Karl Malden has won both an Oscar and an Emmy.*

Year of the Ram

WITH MORE THAN FOUR DECADES of design experience, Clarence Lee has brought his skill and imagination to countless artistic projects. But his design for this eleventh stamp in the award-winning Lunar New Year series is particularly meaningful: it reminds him of his family.

"One of the blessings of the Lunar New Year stamp series is the fun of relating the characteristics of each animal to the personality of people born under that sign," he explains. "My wife and twin granddaughters were born during the Year of the Ram, and their sign calls for them to be gentle, compassionate, and artistic—which is so true of the three dearest people in my life."

Since 1992, when he designed the Year of the Rooster stamp, Lee has incorporated a tradition of paper-cut art from central China to sustain a consistent approach across the entire Lunar New Year series. In doing so, he found that delving into venerable traditions can lead to profound thoughts about the role of different cultures in American life.

"Through my research into Chinese history, I learned of the great sacrifices my

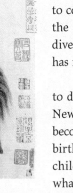

ancestors made for the next generation," he says, "and I realized that all Americans have stories of someone braving hardships to come across the sea, whether they came from the West or the East. We are a nation of immigrants, and I believe that diversity is what has provided the strength and tolerance that has made our country so unique in the world."

Lee has been delighted to discover that the Lunar New Year stamps have become frequent gifts for birthdays and for newborn children, and he enjoys what he calls "an endless procession of people who want me to sign stamps for their family and friends." But the popularity of these stamps has also given him a greater appreciation for the joy that all Americans can feel when they observe traditional celebrations.

"It has so much more relevance to me now that I understand and see the pride in our culture," he says. "It's the same pride that people in every culture should hold in their hearts for their ancestors."

ABOVE LEFT: This ink drawing from the late 13th or early 14th century is in the collection of the Freer Gallery in Washington, D.C. ABOVE RIGHT: A 15th-century woodcut. BELOW RIGHT: An enormous dragon looms over a Shanghai garden. FACING PAGE: People born in the Year of the Ram are said to be fond of nature and are often happiest in a tranquil and secure environment.

Place and Date of Issue
Chicago, IL   January 15, 2003

Artist and Designer
Clarence Lee

Art Director
Terrence W. McCaffrey

Thurgood Marshall

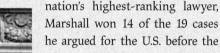

WHEN THURGOOD MARSHALL died in 1993, he left behind a monumental legacy: a brilliant career marked by a commitment to defending constitutional rights and affirmative action. In a eulogy delivered at the Supreme Court, Chief Justice William H. Rehnquist clearly articulated Marshall's influence on American society.

"Inscribed above the front entrance to this Court building are the words 'Equal Justice Under Law,'" Rehnquist said. "Surely no individual did more to make these words a reality than Thurgood Marshall."

Born in Baltimore, Maryland, in 1908, Marshall graduated from Lincoln University in 1930 and then in 1933 from Howard University Law School, where he was first in his class. He soon rose through the ranks of the National Association for the Advancement of Colored People (NAACP), becoming the first director-counsel of the NAACP Legal Defense and Education Fund and winning numerous high-profile victories. In 1954, he and his legal team prevailed in the landmark Supreme Court case, *Brown v. Board of Education of Topeka, Kansas,* which struck down segregation in public schools.

In 1961, President Kennedy appointed Marshall to the U.S. Court of Appeals for the Second Circuit. Four years later, President Johnson appointed him the first African-American solicitor general of the United States. As the

nation's highest-ranking lawyer, Marshall won 14 of the 19 cases he argued for the U.S. before the Supreme Court.

Marshall made history again in 1967, when he was sworn in as the first African-American justice of the U.S. Supreme Court. The photograph on this stamp, taken that same year by Abdon Daoud Ackad, Sr., depicts Marshall just as he began his remarkable and highly influential 24-year tenure.

"It's a wonderful photo of him at the height of his career," says designer Richard Sheaff of this 26th stamp in the Black Heritage series. "We looked at a number of different options, including a variety of photographic portraits and even a painting, but this one was from just the right stage in his life, and it was consistent with the other striking black-and-white photos we've used in this series for many years now."

Ackad, who died in 1981, was known for his portraits of notable American figures, and philatelists will be intrigued to know that his photograph of Senator Robert A. Taft formed the basis for a commemorative stamp in 1960. However, most Americans see Ackad's work every day in another widespread and highly collectible medium: his portrait of Franklin D. Roosevelt was used to create the engraving on the U.S. dime.

FACING PAGE: *This portrait by Simmie Knox is part of the collection of the U.S. Supreme Court.* RIGHT: *A determined Marshall stands outside the Supreme Court in August 1958.*

Place and Date of Issue	Photographer	Designer and Art Director
Washington, DC January 7, 2003	**Abdon Daoud Ackad, Sr.**	**Richard Sheaff**

Love

EVER SINCE THE FIRST LOVE stamps were issued by the U.S. Postal Service in 1973, collectors and the general public alike have eagerly sought them out, welcoming the opportunity to grace their love letters, wedding invitations, or holiday wishes with stylish and colorful designs.

The first stamp in the long-running series featured the work of pop artist Robert Indiana, whose iconic design of the word "Love" has appeared in a wide variety of settings, including a popular sculpture at Kennedy Plaza in Philadelphia, "the city of brotherly love." Subsequent stamps have included other modern designs, including abstract decorations and rainbows, as well as more traditional elements such as Renaissance cherubs and Victorian lace. Each previous Love stamp is a reminder of that year's particular sentiments and styles, a unique and indispensable part of the cards and letters that have carried some of our fondest memories.

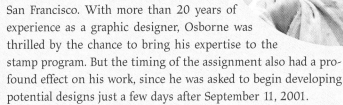

With this new design, the U.S. Postal Service returns to the colorful roots of the series with eye-catching artwork by Michael Osborne of San Francisco. With more than 20 years of experience as a graphic designer, Osborne was thrilled by the chance to bring his expertise to the stamp program. But the timing of the assignment also had a profound effect on his work, since he was asked to begin developing potential designs just a few days after September 11, 2001.

"In light of the horrific events that took place only a week earlier, I put everything I had into designing the Love stamp," says Osborne. "Once I started, the emotions I felt fueled the creative process. After two weeks, I had so many designs that I had to spend several days trying to determine which stamps should be presented."

The warmth and exuberance of Osborne's approach to the Love stamp impressed art director Ethel Kessler, who submitted fourteen of his designs to the Citizens' Stamp Advisory Committee. The committee was delighted by Osborne's artwork—and Kessler says that some of his designs may be considered for future stamp issuances as well.

"Michael's work was fresh in every way," she says, "and very playful in the best sense."

Place and Date of Issue	Artist and Designer	Art Director
Atlantic City, NJ August 16, 2002	**Michael Osborne**	**Ethel Kessler**

Cinematography

Costume Design

AMERICAN FILMMAKING
Behind the Scenes

WHEN ART DIRECTOR Ethel Kessler recalls her work on the American Filmmaking stamp pane, she's quick to point out that a photo of Cecil B. DeMille, known for his undeniably epic productions, was the perfect choice to adorn the selvage.

"These stamps are a great example of 'years in the making and a cast of thousands,'" she says with a laugh. "Researchers, librarians, writers, designers, proofreaders, and others—it took a surprising number of people to get this design just right."

To create these new stamps, which honor all of those multitalented, highly skilled men and women who work behind the scenes to create movie magic, Kessler knew that she needed to involve designers who were intimately familiar with filmmaking. Following a recommendation from a colleague, she contacted Imaginary Forces, a Los Angeles design firm renowned for its award-winning film title sequences. After meeting with Kyle Cooper, the firm's creative director and managing partner, she was confident that they were the right team for the job.

Sound

"At Imaginary Forces, they're very involved in the film industry," Kessler explains, "so they understand better than anyone how to translate graphic interpretations into the medium of film. In this case, what they needed to do was pare down the visuals to their absolute essence, making each image interesting and giving some symmetry to the entire stamp pane. It was a big task."

Cooper agrees, noting that a major challenge in designing this stamp pane was figuring out exactly what to show on each stamp.

"Our initial work entailed extensive archival research for the perfect images," he says. "This was the hardest part of the assignment

ABOVE, LEFT TO RIGHT: *Capturing the colors and contours of the desert in* Lawrence of Arabia. *Audrey Hepburn, elegantly costumed. Onstage singers and a multitude of offstage technicians make the 1943 film* This Is the Army. *A boy and his alien prepare to take flight in E.T. The Extra-Terrestrial. LEFT: Meryl Streep and Gene Hackman play actors behind the scenes in* Postcards from the Edge.

Place and Date of Issue
Beverly Hills, CA   February 25, 2003

Designer
Imaginary Forces

Art Director
Ethel Kessler

14

FILMMAKING   07   006   FILMMAKING   05   005   04   BEHIND THE SCENES 04   003   FILMMAKING

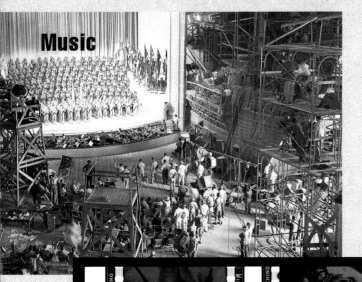

Music

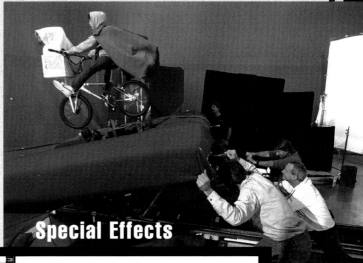

Special Effects

SCREENWRITING

DIRECTING

COSTUME DESIGN

MUSIC

MAKEUP

ART DIRECTION

CINEMATOGRAPHY

FILM EDITING

SPECIAL EFFECTS

SOUND

AMERICAN
FILM MAKING:
BEHIND the SCENES

"Thousands and thousands of details...
go into the making of a film. It is the sum
total of all these things that either
makes a great picture or destroys it."

DAVID O. SELZNICK, Producer

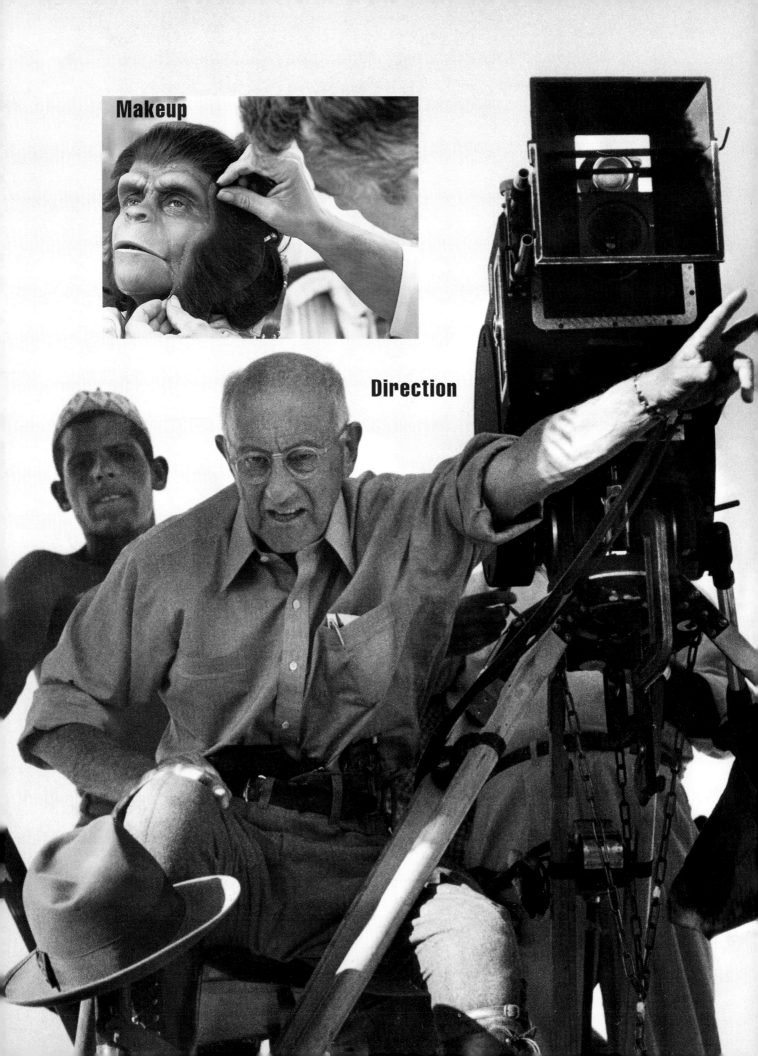

Makeup

Direction

Art Direction

and the one that required the most time. Our task entailed locating images that expressed the magic and power of each of the crafts within the medium."

However, inspiration struck when Cooper and his staff decided to follow up on a hunch, and soon their direction was clear.

"We wondered what the stamps would look like as frames from an actual film, so we went to our vault and took out a strip of film. To our surprise, the frame size was almost the same size as the stamp we were designing. This is when the project became very exciting to us."

Cooper knows from working within the industry that making a film requires the vision and expertise of scores of artists and technicians who collaborate to bring their collective vision to life. As a result, he's proud to have played such a prominent role in a stamp project that recognizes the accomplishments of Hollywood's behind-the-scenes talents.

"For years I have been designing film title sequences, working with some of the finest directors in the world," he says, "so these stamps have allowed me an opportunity to thank them in a small and circumspect way."

Cooper adds that this project holds another personal connection for him: He studied design under Bradbury Thompson, the brilliant and prolific graphic artist who designed more than 120 stamps and who served as design coordinator of the Citizens' Stamp Advisory Committee from 1969 to 1978.

"I designed speculative stamps as a student, so I found it exceedingly gratifying to be involved in an actual commissioned stamp design," Cooper says, pointing out that envisioning designs for the big screen has more in common with small-scale stamp design than most people may suspect.

"Like our other, larger work, this project demanded extensive research to define and solve a specific challenge. What we brought to it was our expertise in telling a story in one frame or sequence—condensing time, and the story of each field of filmmaking expertise, into a single, powerful image."

FACING PAGE: *Cecil B. DeMille points the way for Moses in his 1956 epic* The Ten Commandments. INSET: *A makeup artist readies a patient inhabitant of* Planet of the Apes. ABOVE: *Perry Ferguson completes a sketch for* Citizen Kane. BELOW LEFT: *A script page from* Gone with the Wind. BELOW RIGHT: *J. Watson Webb, Jr., in 1946, editing* The Razor's Edge.

Screenwriting

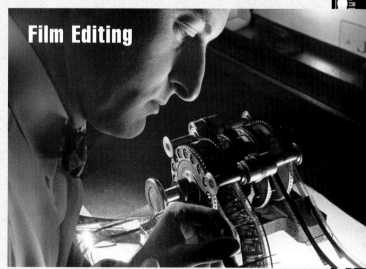
Film Editing

Ohio Statehood

CARVED FROM THE VAST NORTHWEST Territory in 1803, Ohio has been the birthplace of seven presidents and has also produced some of the nation's greatest scientific and technological pioneers. But capturing the essence of the diverse state in a single image proved tricky—until art director Phil Jordan came across the photography of Ian Adams, whose work beautifully depicts the distinctive landscape and contours of the Buckeye State.

Based in Cuyahoga Falls, Adams has been a contributing editor of *Ohio Magazine* since 1989, and his photographs have appeared in numerous books and magazines. A veteran environmental photographer, he knew that a favorite scenic overlook a few miles north of Marietta would offer a picturesque view on a beautiful autumn morning.

"The barn and silos of the small farm next to the country road," he says, "with the rolling foothills of the Appalachians in the distance, hillsides glowing with deep fall color in the early morning mid-October sunlight—it all evinced a strong sense of place in this pastoral hill country of southeast Ohio."

No stranger to travel, Adams is often on the road looking for other iconic images like this one to represent unique American scenes.

"As a full-time environmental photographer, I spend part of each year traveling throughout Ohio and other eastern U.S. states searching for evocative photographs of natural, rural, architectural, and historical areas," he says, esti-

mating that he drives nearly 25,000 miles annually in pursuit of that goal. But when he comes home, he comes home to Ohio.

"About half of my time is spent on Ohio-related photography projects," Adams says, "and most of the seven books I've had published are on Ohio subjects. I enjoy promoting the Buckeye State through my photography, so having one of my images selected for the Ohio stamp is a special honor."

LEFT: *Sunset over Lake Erie, with the famous Lorain Lighthouse in the distance.* ABOVE RIGHT: *This hand-colored woodcut depicts border settlers building a log cabin.* BELOW RIGHT: *One of Ohio's many painted "bicentennial barns."* FACING PAGE: *An idyllic scene in a 1939 painting by Charles Burchfield.* INSET: *Autumn in Holmes County.*

Place and Date of Issue	Photographer	Designer and Art Director
Chillicothe, OH March 1, 2003	**Ian Adams**	**Phil Jordan**

NATIONAL
WILDLIFE
REFUGE
SYSTEM

Pelican Island National Wildlife Refuge

IT ALL BEGAN WITH A SMALL three-acre island in the Indian River Lagoon on the east coast of central Florida. Established on March 14, 1903, by executive order of President Theodore Roosevelt, Pelican Island National Wildlife Refuge was the first official wildlife refuge in the United States. Its creation marks the beginning of the National Wildlife Refuge System, which today encompasses more than 93 million acres across more than 570 refuges and wetland management districts.

Pelican Island has undergone significant changes in the last hundred years. In addition to the three acres of the island itself, the refuge has grown to include 5,377 acres consisting largely of submerged lands, mangrove islands, and marshes. Hundreds of species of fish, birds, plants, and mammals live within the refuge, including some that have been listed by the federal government as threatened or endangered.

But despite the refuge's monumental historical and ecological importance, depicting it on a stamp presented a significant design challenge.

"I tried, but I found it impossible to show the actual island," explains art director Carl T. Herrman. "It's very small and without significant landmarks." As a result, Herrman says he decided to focus on one defining aspect of the refuge: the pelican itself.

"I worked up a design featuring a gorgeous John James Audubon painting of a brown pelican. I also developed concepts using various photos of pelicans. I used to live in Florida beside a nature preserve, so I appreciate these magnificent and comical birds."

This final, approved design consists of a photograph by James Brandt of a brown pelican, *Pelecanus occidentalis*. Although numerous other animal species, including the American white pelican, now enjoy the protection of the refuge, Pelican Island was originally intended to protect the last breeding grounds for brown pelicans along Florida's east coast. Herrman says that by depicting the brown pelican, this stamp emphasizes the humble history of an island that inaugurated our vast and indispensable national refuge system.

"The Brandt photo fits the format perfectly," he adds, "and it also makes a really nice ornithological portrait."

FACING PAGE: *Pelicans at sunset.* INSET: *Kofa National Wildlife Refuge in Arizona was established in 1939.* ABOVE LEFT: *Covering nearly 700 square miles in Georgia and northern Florida, Okefenokee National Wildlife Refuge is home to many plants and animals.* ABOVE RIGHT: *Pelicans have inspired a century of refuge and preservation efforts.*

Place and Date of Issue	Photographer	Designer and Art Director
Sebastian, FL March 14, 2003	**James Brandt**	**Carl T. Herrman**

Cesar E. Chavez

CESAR E. CHAVEZ IS BEST REMEMBERED as the founder of the United Farm Workers of America, AFL-CIO (UFW). A strong believer in the principles of nonviolence, he effectively employed peaceful tactics such as fasts, boycotts, strikes, and pilgrimages. "He was the champion for hardworking but underpaid workers," says art director Carl T. Herrman, who designed this new stamp honoring Chavez. "His life shows that you don't have to be a wealthy person to make a difference in America."

For more than three decades, Chavez led the first successful farm workers union in American history, achieving gains such as fair wages, medical coverage, pension benefits, and humane living conditions. However, Chavez's work transcended any one movement or cause. He inspired millions of Americans to seek social justice and civil rights for the poor and disenfranchised. He advocated for nonviolent social reform. He was an environmentalist and labor leader. Ultimately, he forged an extraordinary and diverse national coalition of students, middle-class consumers, trade unionists, religious groups, women, and minorities.

Basing his stamp design around a 1976 photograph of Chavez, Herrman added rows of crops to the background, but he was not entirely satisfied with the idea of a photo montage. Doing justice to the subject required something extra, so Herrman called upon painter Robert Rodriguez to bring the design to life.

"Robert is one of my favorite artists," he says. "We worked together on the Cinco de Mayo stamp and the Celebrate The Century series, and he did an amazing portrait for this stamp."

Rodriguez, who lives in Pasadena, California, brought his own observations and experience to the stamp art. "I've been to some of the areas where Chavez worked, and I remembered what the light was like. I showed the fields in the hazy afternoon sun, so that the scene was set back and Chavez was brought forward more strongly in the design."

Rodriguez says that he also had definite ideas about how to approach the portrait. "I wanted the Chavez artwork not to be as slick or polished as some other work I've done; I wanted a more natural quality to the painting. I had early American painting in mind, but I think the artwork has a little bit in common with the style of Mexican painter Diego Rivera, too."

Herrman and Rodriguez were both especially pleased that the stamp passed the most crucial test—with the people who knew Chavez best.

"It was presented to the Cesar E. Chavez Foundation and the Chavez family," says Herrman. "The finest compliment was to receive their approval."

LEFT: *Chavez inspired millions to seek justice and civil rights.*
ABOVE: *Chavez marches in Sacramento, 1966.* FACING PAGE: *Senator Robert F. Kennedy called Chavez "one of the heroic figures of our time."*

Place and Date of Issue
Los Angeles, CA   April 23, 2003

Artist
Robert Rodriguez

Designer and Art Director
Carl T. Herrman

Zora Neale Hurston

Jordan, who has been flying gliders since 1979, felt strongly that this momentous event had to be depicted by an artist who was also a sport pilot. Fortunately, he found a kindred spirit in designer and illustrator McRay Magleby.

"We both owned numerous reference books on the subject," Jordan says, "so we discussed only the event, without any references to how the art would look."

Jordan was pleased by his decision to let Magleby follow his own artistic instincts. "McRay's art portrays simply and beautifully what I think are perhaps the most significant twelve seconds of any century," he says. "He has invoked that first feeling of momentary freedom from the earth that gives every flier a shared bond."

This project also allowed Jordan to follow up on one question that had been nagging him for years: what the weather had been like on that historic December day in 1903.

"I had seen countless illustrations of the first flight that depict stormy cumulonimbus clouds swirling around a dark sky, which is a reasonable assumption for December on the Outer Banks," he says. "But many years of scrutinizing the photographs of December 17, 1903, convinced me that the very hard and defined shadows cast in all the photos just had to indicate otherwise."

Since neither of the Wright brothers ever stated what the cloud cover was like on that day, or whether it was even sunny or overcast, Jordan decided to investigate.

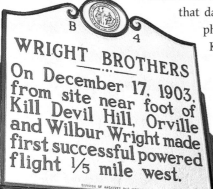

"I asked our research group to obtain weather information for that day. Through the National Oceanic and Atmospheric Administration, we obtained photocopies of the actual weather reports filed in 1903 by Joseph J. Dosher of the Kitty Hawk weather station."

The revelations in these century-old documents brought blue skies for Jordan, who was thrilled to learn that his suspicions had been confirmed.

"In the report for December 17," he says with a smile, "the number of clouds in the sky is zero—and the 'state of the weather' is indicated as clear."

FACING PAGE: *The Wrights on their front porch in Dayton, 1909.* TOP: *The 1902 Wright glider in action at Kill Devil Hills.* ABOVE: *This special newspaper supplement welcomed the Wrights home to Dayton in 1909.*

Louisiana Purchase

THE LOUISIANA PURCHASE, which doubled the size of the United States with the stroke of a pen, is often referred to as the greatest real estate deal in history. Our country became one of the largest in the world, and the heartland of the continent was opened to American exploration and settlement—at a final cost of about four cents an acre.

When the United States purchased the vast area of land from France in 1803, no one, including the French, knew just how far north and west it stretched. But a territorial government was established in 1804, and westward expansion began immediately. For the millions of Americans who now live in Louisiana and the twelve other states that were carved from the immense territory, the bicentennial of the Louisiana Purchase commemorates not only a key event in American history, but also a defining moment in the history of the places they call home.

Stamp artist Garin Baker, who lives and works in New Windsor, New York, literally finds himself at home in history, too.

"I'm a bit of a history buff," Baker explains, "and I'm interested in historical houses. I spend some of my free time traveling to historical sites, especially in my local area, the Hudson River Valley in upstate New York, where I have renovated a 1790 stone house, carriage house, and barn as my home and studio space."

For Baker, bringing his own style to the artwork that appears in the foreground of the Louisiana Purchase stamp meant exploring several historical illustrations. After consultation with art director Richard Sheaff, he based his painting on a half-tone

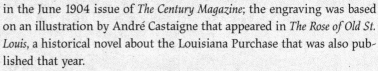

engraving published in the June 1904 issue of *The Century Magazine*; the engraving was based on an illustration by André Castaigne that appeared in *The Rose of Old St. Louis*, a historical novel about the Louisiana Purchase that was also published that year.

As an artist who has produced more than 300 book covers, Baker was intrigued by these century-old illustrations. But he is also an accomplished landscape painter, and he says that an older artistic tradition informs his art, one that made him ideally suited to work on the Louisiana Purchase stamp.

"I spend a great deal of my working time painting in the spirit of the Hudson River School," he says, citing the 19th-century landscape painters whose art inspires him. "In a way, you could say that these great artists were responding to the inspiration and vision behind the Louisiana Purchase and the idea of Manifest Destiny."

ABOVE LEFT: *The expanded United States in 1804.* ABOVE RIGHT: *This ornate volume, now in the National Archives, includes financial agreements between France and the United States.* FACING PAGE: *President Thomas Jefferson persuaded Congress to approve the treaty allowing for the purchase of Louisiana.*

Place and Date of Issue	Artist	Designer and Art Director
New Orleans, LA April 30, 2003	**Garin Baker**	**Richard Sheaff**

Treaty

Between the United States

and the French Republic

The President of the United States of...

...onsul of the French Republic in the na...

...eople desiring to remove all Source of misun...

...lative to objects of discussion mentioned in...

...nd fifth article of the Convention of the [8th] [30...

...lative to the rights claimed by the United Stat...

...e Treaty concluded at Madrid the 27 of October 179...

...is Catholic Majesty, & the said United States, & willing...

...rengthen the union and friendship which at the...

...he said Convention was happily reestablished bet...

...ations have respectively named their Plenipot...

...The President of the United States, by and ...

...nd consent of the Senate of the said States; ...

...Livingston Minister Plenipotentiary o...

...nd James Monroe Minister Plen...

...traordinary of the said State...

...rench Republic; An...

...f the French people...

...Minister of the pu...

...ly exchanged thei...

Mary Cassatt

Mary Cassatt

AS ART DIRECTOR for the American Treasures series, Derry Noyes is always looking for superb examples of American art that would also make graceful and elegant commemorative stamps. But when it came time to work on this year's issuance, she had to look no further than her own studio.

"We needed art that was colorful, visually appealing, and which could truly be called a treasure," she says. "I had been working with Mary Cassatt paintings for another project, but they fit the requirements of American Treasures so well that I decided to use them for that series instead."

Known especially for her figure studies and engaging portraits of mothers and children, Cassatt was the only American ever invited to exhibit with the French Impressionists. Born in Pennsylvania in 1844, she attended the Pennsylvania Academy of the Fine Arts in Philadelphia and continued her studies in Europe, settling permanently in Paris in the mid-1870s.

Recurring themes in Cassatt's paintings, pastels, prints, and etchings include children engaging in various pastimes and contemporary women pursuing everyday activities such as entertaining visitors, reading, and caring for children. Paying careful attention to naturalistic pose and gesture, she developed a vigorous, innovative style and rendered her domestic subjects with a refreshingly unsentimental intimacy.

"The four works of art on these stamps relate to each other quite well," says Noyes. "They all have similar colors, and the subject matter—mothers and children—is also very appealing."

Inaugurated in 2001 with the Amish Quilts stamp pane, the American Treasures series is intended to showcase beautiful works of American fine arts and crafts. With this year's issuance, Noyes has taken an approach that not only highlights a great artist, but also familiarizes even more Americans with some of that artist's masterworks.

"It was a nice, new turn for the series to take," she says, adding that collectors and casual stamp-buyers who like these stamps should keep an expectant eye on the American Treasures series in coming years.

"Future subjects may include more fine art," she says, "and it's always possible that we'll see other types of American treasures, too, perhaps examples of folk art and sculpture. One thing is certain: they're going to look really beautiful on envelopes."

FACING PAGE: *An 1897 pastel drawing by Cassatt.* ABOVE LEFT: *A photograph of Cassatt during the early 1900s.* RIGHT: The Kiss, *dated 1890-91, from The Art Institute of Chicago.*

Place and Date of Issue	Artist	Designer and Art Director
Columbus, OH August 7, 2003	**Mary Cassatt**	**Derry Noyes**

Southeastern Lighthouses

SOME SUBJECTS are regular fixtures in the life of an artist; for Howard Koslow, one of those subjects is undoubtedly lighthouses.

"I live near several popular New Jersey lighthouses, such as Barnegat Light, Sandy Hook, and Cape May," Koslow says, "and I've done a few gallery paintings of lighthouses, as well as the Lighthouses stamp series. I think they've simply become a subject that people associate with me as an artist."

Koslow, who served as artist for two previous lighthouse stamp booklets, has been creating artwork for the U.S. Postal Service since 1971. With his focus on architectural and historical subjects and his reputation for accuracy, he was once again the natural choice when art director Howard Paine learned that the Postal Service intended to issue five new stamps in its popular lighthouses series.

"Howard is a great painter and an old pro," says Paine, who has known and worked with Koslow for more than 30 years. "He does a ton of his own research, too. Often when he comes across relevant articles about subjects we're work-

ing on, he clips them and sends them to me with red notations. He's very thorough, and it shows in his work."

For the Southeastern Lighthouses stamps, Paine and Koslow decided to rethink their usual approach. One of the first ideas they considered was designing these stamps as horizontal rather than vertical—a radical departure from previous lighthouses issuances and a concept that Paine says was not destined for success.

"At first, Howard and I thought it might be a nice opportunity to show more landscape," Paine says, "but then we realized that each lighthouse would be miniscule. They would have been only a quarter of an inch tall on the final printed stamps."

Once Koslow and Paine decided to keep the vertical format, they weighed their options. They soon agreed on a subtle way to make each of the five new stamps a bit more dynamic.

TOP LEFT: *The powerful lantern at Hillsboro Island Lighthouse.* LEFT: *Morris Island Lighthouse is a Charleston landmark.* ABOVE RIGHT: *At Virginia Beach, visitors can see not only Old Cape Henry Lighthouse, but also the distinctive black-and-white lighthouse that replaced it.* FACING PAGE: *Tybee Island Lighthouse in Georgia.*

Place and Date of Issue	Artist	Designer and Art Director
Tybee Island, GA June 13, 2003	**Howard Koslow**	**Howard E. Paine**

34

"We wanted a second element in each design," Koslow says. "Our purpose was to make each stamp more of a picture rather than just an architectural rendering. That's why we added a sailboat, or a fishing boat, or some other detail that gives the viewer a nice sense of place."

But these new design details brought an added challenge for Koslow and Paine: ensuring that the artwork still accurately represented each lighthouse's surroundings.

"For Morris Island, we had to do a lot of checking," Koslow explains. "At first I had a little shrimp boat right in front of the lighthouse, but the Coast Guard assured us that it would never be able to get that close. So now we've put the boat behind the lighthouse, in an area where the water would be deep enough."

Later, long after Paine and Koslow thought they were finished with their work, they found they had an entirely different problem with Tybee Island—resulting from the fact that Postal Service artists often work several years in advance of a stamp's issuance.

"I had been down in that area right outside of Savannah recently," says Koslow. "I took some photographs of the lighthouse. I then made my painting, and I thought everything was fine—until we discovered that they had changed part of the lighthouse's paint scheme!" Koslow was quick to make the last-minute change. "It's important to me that the artwork is accurate."

As art director for these attractive new stamps, Paine says that he's pleased by their high level of accuracy, but he's especially gratified by the public's enthusiastic response to lighthouses and everything associated with them.

"People love them," he says. "They're beautiful to look at, and they're also rich in history. There are few structures that are as beloved, and I think Howard's paintings certainly capture their appeal."

FACING PAGE: *Cape Lookout Lighthouse in North Carolina was automated in 1950.* FACING PAGE INSET: *Morris Island has weathered hurricanes, a major earthquake, and the total erosion of the surrounding land.* LEFT: *An example of a Fresnel lens, used in many American lighthouses after 1850.* ABOVE: *A view of Morris Island Lighthouse from Folly Beach, South Carolina.*

Korean War Veterans Memorial

DEDICATED IN 1995, the Korean War Veterans Memorial in Washington, D.C., is a touchstone for those who were affected by the conflict. Featuring 19 stainless-steel statues that depict American troops on patrol in a wedge formation, the memorial also includes a Pool of Remembrance and a granite wall etched with images of those who served—all elements that provide a place of solemn remembrance for the war's numerous veterans.

Photographer John W. Alli, who served as a second lieutenant in the U.S. Marine Corps during Desert Storm, knows how profound those memories can be. With the dramatic photograph that appears on this stamp, Alli intended to honor the experiences of all Korean War veterans, but one particular veteran was foremost in his mind.

"I took this photo with the purpose of giving it to my father for his retirement ceremony," he says. "He served as a machine gunner with the Marines during the Korean War, and he was a U.S. State Department employee for almost 40 years."

Hoping to convey the bitter cold of a Korean winter, Alli drove to the memorial in his four-wheel-drive truck during the blizzard that hit Washington in January 1996. Forced to hike the last mile through the snow, he arrived at the memorial before dawn and set up for the shot. Alli says that the experience was a moving reminder of the veterans' sacrifices.

"As I waited in the dark, freezing weather for the first light of dawn I thought, 'This is nothing compared to what the Korean War veterans had to endure.' At the first hint of light I began taking a series of photographs."

Alli was especially pleased by a photo he dubbed "Real Life," and the first print, signed and framed, went to his father for his retirement ceremony. The photo later became the basis for this stamp, issued on the 50th anniversary of the 1953 armistice that ended the hostilities.

The following year, when he returned to photograph the memorial during the summer, Alli met another Korean War veteran for whom the memorial was an intensely personal place of remembrance.

"He had traveled from Missouri to plant an American flag next to the statue of the squad leader. The flag was to honor his platoon commander in Korea, who had saved the platoon and in doing so paid the ultimate price."

Later, Alli sent the veteran a copy of the photograph that now appears on this stamp. "It was the least I could do for an American who fought for our country and who knew the meaning of 'all gave some, and some gave all.'"

ABOVE LEFT: *Statues at the memorial depict American troops in the Army, the Marines, the Navy, and the Air Force.* ABOVE RIGHT: *Nearly 37,000 Americans died in Korea and more than 103,000 were wounded.* FACING PAGE: *Korean War veterans who visit the memorial are frequently impressed by the incredible level of authenticity in each statue.*

Place and Date of Issue
Washington, DC   July 27, 2003

Photographer
John W. Alli

Designer and Art Director
Richard Sheaff

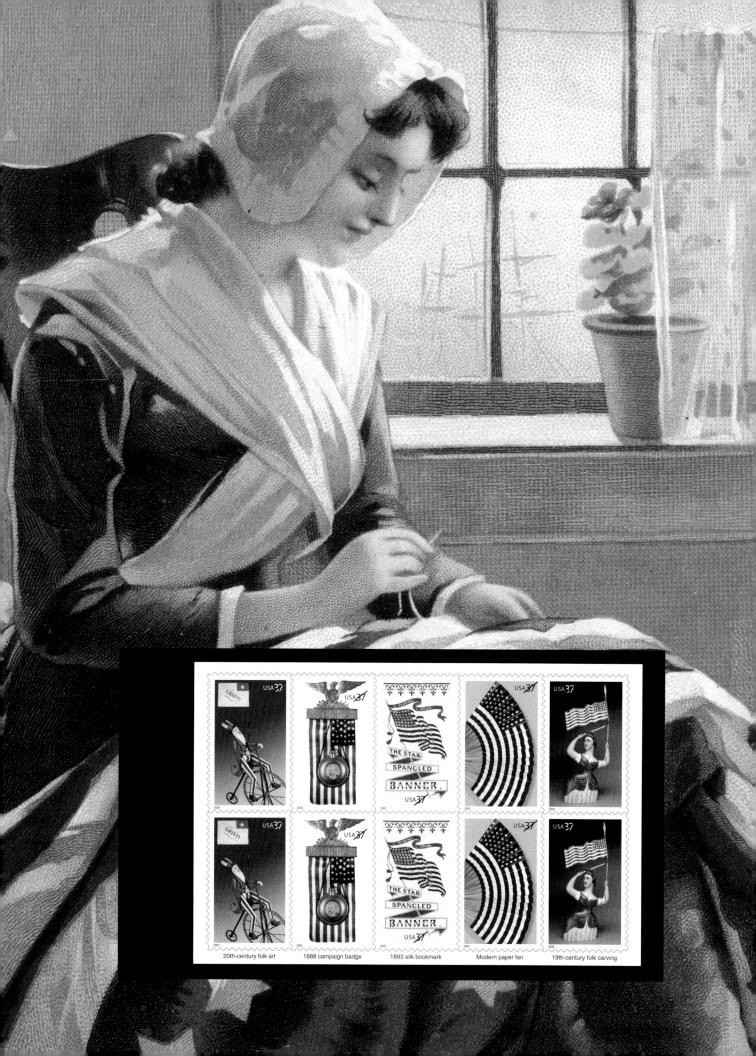

20th-century folk art   1888 campaign badge   1893 silk bookmark   Modern paper fan   19th-century folk carving

Old Glory

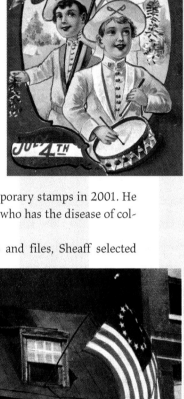

FROM POSTCARDS AND ADVERTISEMENTS to guitar straps, playing cards, and children's puzzles, the red, white, and blue of the Stars and Stripes have graced virtually every aspect of American culture since the nation's first official flag was authorized in 1777. When the U.S. Postal Service decided to issue a prestige booklet with five stamps featuring patriotic ephemera inspired by the American flag, Richard Sheaff knew he was the right art director for the job.

No stranger to flag stamps, Sheaff designed the striking Stars and Stripes stamp pane issued in 2000, as well as more than 200 other U.S. stamps. But when he needed star-spangled items for this new project, he knew exactly where to look: his own home.

"I've spent 30 years collecting ephemera, so it was logical for me to do it," says Sheaff, who also owns the chromolithographs of Santa Claus that appeared on the Holiday Contemporary stamps in 2001. He adds with a laugh: "I'm one of those people who has the disease of collecting anything and everything."

After rummaging through his boxes and files, Sheaff selected three colorful and engaging items: the top portion of a silk bookmark that was woven at the Columbian Exposition in Chicago in 1893, an example of 20th-century folk art featuring Uncle Sam riding a high-wheel bicycle, and a modern folding fan with a flag design. For the remaining two stamps, he chose items from other collections: a 19th-century hand-painted carving of a woman proudly holding aloft a sword and flag, and an 1888 presidential campaign badge with a photograph of Benjamin Harrison.

What strikes Sheaff most about these items is how well they document the changing ways in which Americans have conceived of their young country.

"These national symbols have been used for a number of different purposes," he explains. "Originally, symbols such as an eagle, a stylized allegorical woman, or Uncle Sam were used to represent the country much more

FACING PAGE: *This scene from an old insurance calendar shows Betsy Ross sewing the American flag.* ABOVE RIGHT: *A delightful antique greeting card celebrating Independence Day.* RIGHT: *The Betsy Ross house in Philadelphia, in a circa 1913 photo.*

Place and Date of Issue
New York, NY   April 3, 2003

Designer and Art Director
Richard Sheaff

often than the flag was." For example, Sheaff says that the carving of the woman with the flag is a fine example of a female personification of the U.S., sometimes known as "Columbia" or "Liberty," that has been popular with folk artists since the nation's beginning.

Sheaff points out that although the flag has a long history in American life, it became the definitive symbol of the United States only at the end of the nineteenth century.

"The flag first became really prominent around the time of the Civil War, when it was used by the North," he says. Afterwards, advances in printing and publishing techniques helped to keep the image of the flag always in sight, especially through color advertising and varied ephemera such as the items that appear on these stamps.

Why has the design of the Stars and Stripes remained such a powerful and resilient symbol? Sheaff believes it's because the design is, in its own way, a work of American genius.

"The flag is used all the time to invoke the grandeur of the country, but I think part of its success is that it's just a great symbol; it really catches the eye. Beyond what it represents, it's undeniably a very bold graphic pattern."

ABOVE: *This scene from a circa 1915 postcard sends a patriotic message from children at a New York City nursery.* LEFT: *This woman wears her patriotism, circa 1908.* RIGHT: *This wooden gate from Jefferson County, New York, is dated circa 1876.* FACING PAGE: *A stirring symbol of home and country.*

ARCTIC TUNDRA

FIFTH IN A SERIES

NATURE OF AMERICA

Arctic Tundra

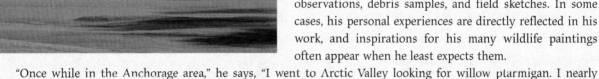

LONG BEFORE ARTIST John D. Dawson ever saw the arctic tundra in person, he had already fallen in love with this beautiful and fragile ecosystem—through photographs.

"My first close look at the arctic tundra was many years ago," he says, fondly recalling his initial journeys through the pages of books and magazines. "While gathering information for an Audubon Society poster to inform citizens of the importance and beauty of the arctic wilderness, I became hooked on this amazing place, even though I had never been there. It was fascinating just to know it existed."

With this fifth stamp pane in the Nature of America series, Dawson depicts an autumn tundra scene in the northern foothills of the majestic Brooks Range in Alaska. In this coldest of the North American ecosystems, the soil is permanently frozen except for the surface layer, thawed by the summer sun, where plants take root. The frozen soil, or permafrost, keeps the surface layer moist by preventing water from seeping deeply into the ground. Arctic plants have adapted to survive the cold and wind: most grow close to the ground, many are evergreen, and all are frost hardy.

To illustrate the diversity of the species found in this vast treeless region in northern Alaska and Canada, Dawson's detailed acrylic painting includes 24 types of plants and animals—a revelation to anyone who thinks of the tundra as hostile and brutally uninhabitable.

Dawson, who now lives in Hawaii, has made several trips to the arctic tundra since he first researched its amazing plants and animals, and his sharp eye and painstaking attention to detail are evident in this stamp pane. Although he uses extensive research, specimen studies, and interviews with experts, Dawson also relies on his own recorded field observations, debris samples, and field sketches. In some cases, his personal experiences are directly reflected in his work, and inspirations for his many wildlife paintings often appear when he least expects them.

"Once while in the Anchorage area," he says, "I went to Arctic Valley looking for willow ptarmigan. I nearly jumped out of my skin as four flushed from right under my feet."

Luckily, Dawson was quick to respond, and even this spontaneous moment became an experience that he could, with some ingenuity, translate into art.

"I gathered myself fast enough to take four or five photos. I didn't get the sort of close, detailed shot I would have liked—but I was still able to use them in this painting, just below the caribou and above the stream, where you can see them flying away."

FACING PAGE: *Leaves and berries make a brilliant autumn tapestry of red, yellow, and orange.* ABOVE RIGHT: *Pink phlox blossoms brighten the arctic landscape.* ABOVE LEFT: *A stunning August view of Kikitat Mountain in the Arctic National Wildlife Refuge.* RIGHT: *In the fall, grizzly bears fatten before hibernating.*

Place and Date of Issue	Artist	Designer and Art Director
Fairbanks, AK July 2, 2003	**John D. Dawson**	**Ethel Kessler**

District of Columbia

THE MONUMENTS of Washington, D.C., are some of our nation's most recognizable landmarks, iconic symbols of freedom and history that represent American government to the world. But for this stamp honoring the District of Columbia, the U.S. Postal Service looked at our nation's capital from a different perspective, carefully portraying the monuments as important background elements rather than as starring attractions.

A previous stamp celebrating the District of Columbia's 1991 bicentennial showed streetcars and buggies on bustling Pennsylvania Avenue, circa 1903, and this new design needed to stress similar aspects of District life. After all, Washington is more than just a city full of government offices; for more than 500,000 citizens, it's also home.

Art director Ethel Kessler concluded that a collage would be the best approach for such a complex subject; she also knew that the perfect designer for the job would be Greg Berger, whose intricate photo collage appeared on the Frederick Law Olmsted stamp in 1999. Preliminary designs for this new stamp focused on details from the city's scenic monuments, bridges, and parks, but none fully captured the essence of residential D.C. However, the design soon came to life with the addition of a colorful row of Victorian row houses and part of a historic map. A glorious bouquet of cherry blossoms brightened the stamp—just as the real cherry blossoms brighten the city every springtime.

This stamp also includes another clever design feature: its highly unusual diamond shape, which reflects the original boundaries of the District of Columbia. The public will have to look closely at this stamp when they use it on their

envelopes, but like frequent visitors to the District of Columbia, they will discover charming details and signs of community well beyond the monuments and museums that make the city famous.

FACING PAGE: *Monuments such as the General Meade Civil War Memorial are reminders of the District's national importance.* ABOVE LEFT: *DuPont Circle, one of the District of Columbia's many elegant public spaces.* ABOVE RIGHT: *A view of Georgetown, circa 1855.* BELOW RIGHT: *The vibrant Adams Morgan neighborhood, a center of local nightlife.*

Place and Date of Issue	Designer	Art Director
Washington, DC Fall 2003	**Greg Berger**	**Ethel Kessler**

Audrey Hepburn

MOVIE STAR, FASHION ICON, legendary beauty—Audrey Hepburn delighted audiences worldwide with her charm and sophistication. This ninth stamp in the Legends of Hollywood series honors her with a portrait that reflects not only her glamorous public persona, but also the compassion and depth of emotion that defined her remarkably textured life both on and off the silver screen.

Born in Brussels, Belgium, in 1929, Hepburn was the daughter of a Dutch baroness and her British husband. She spent much of her childhood in England, but in 1939 she moved with her mother to the Netherlands. After Germany invaded the Netherlands in May 1940, Hepburn and her family faced many hardships during the five-year Nazi occupation.

After World War II, Hepburn received a ballet scholarship in London. Following a series of modeling jobs, minor stage roles, and small parts in movies, she was hired in 1951 for the title role in the Broadway play *Gigi*. At the same time she was also hired for her first major Hollywood film role, playing a princess in *Roman Holiday*, for which she won an Academy Award for best actress. She subsequently appeared in nearly 30 movies, receiving Academy Award nominations for her performances in *Sabrina*, *The Nun's Story*, *Breakfast at Tiffany's*, and *Wait Until Dark*.

During the late 1980s and early 1990s, Hepburn was also particularly well known for bringing attention to humanitarian causes, especially children's issues, as a goodwill ambassador for UNICEF.

"She spent a lifetime giving of her talent both in film and in real life," says art director Phil Jordan. "That made it difficult for us to decide what stage in her life we were going to depict."

For this daunting task, Jordan chose Michael J. Deas, praising the artist's "tremendous gift for portraying men and woman of evocative character."

Deas has created artwork for numerous stamps, but he describes Hepburn as his most challenging design yet, suggesting that her beauty, like everything about her life, was deeply unique.

"Of all the stamp portraits I've done for the Postal Service," he says, "hers has been one of the most difficult likenesses I've had to capture. I'm not entirely sure why. It may be that her features were so perfect and yet so irregular—a completely inimitable face."

FACING PAGE: *The very embodiment of grace, 1961.* ABOVE: *Hepburn at home with a fawn in 1958.* LEFT: *Hepburn's 1990 tour of Vietnam was only one of her many missions as a UNICEF goodwill ambassador.*

Place and Date of Issue
Los Angeles, CA   June 11, 2003

Artist and Designer
Michael J. Deas

Art Director
Phil Jordan

Early Football Heroes

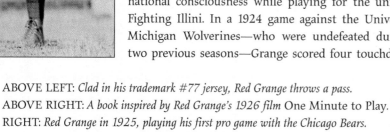

IN RECENT YEARS, the U.S. Postal Service has often tackled the subject of football and its importance to American life, issuing stamps to commemorate legendary coaches, winning teams, and unforgettable games. These new stamps continue this tradition by honoring four amazing players from the early days of the game.

But when designer Richard Sheaff set out to locate the perfect photos, he found that these gridiron greats rarely stood still for the camera.

"We were able to find plenty of photos of them from when they were older," says Sheaff, "but good portraits from their football days—as opposed to shots of them running and jumping where you could barely tell who they were— were hard to come by. What I really wanted was pictures of them looking formidable, as if they had just come off the field."

For WALTER CAMP, known as the father of American football, Sheaff selected a portrait from the famed athlete's college days. Camp played halfback at Yale from 1876 to 1882 and later served as coach and advisor. Deeply involved with the legislative aspects of football until his death in 1925, he is credited with such vital innovations as the system of downs, the restriction to eleven players per side, and the position of quarterback. Camp's alma mater was always first in his heart, which is why this photographic portrait of him at the Yale fence—the sole privilege of team captains—is a fitting representation. "It's also a nice sports photo from that period," adds Sheaff. "You really just don't see great old uniforms like that anymore."

Eagle-eyed football fans will also notice that the 1925 photo on the HAROLD "RED" GRANGE stamp shows "The Galloping Ghost" not in his professional uniform from his days with the Chicago Bears, but in a University of Illinois practice uniform. That's because Grange burst upon the national consciousness while playing for the university's Fighting Illini. In a 1924 game against the University of Michigan Wolverines—who were undefeated during the two previous seasons—Grange scored four touchdowns in

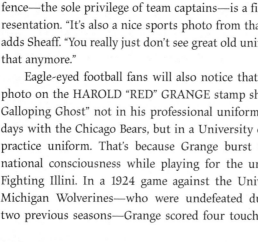

ABOVE LEFT: *Clad in his trademark #77 jersey, Red Grange throws a pass.*
ABOVE RIGHT: *A book inspired by Red Grange's 1926 film* One Minute to Play.
RIGHT: *Red Grange in 1925, playing his first pro game with the Chicago Bears.*
FACING PAGE: *Walter Camp poses at the Yale fence, a privilege of team captains.*

Place and Date of Issue
South Bend, IN   August 8, 2003

Designer and Art Director
Richard Sheaff

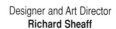

the first 12 minutes of play and ran an incredible 402 yards of offense. When he began playing for the Bears in 1925, his transition from college football brought credibility and publicity to a then-struggling National Football League, and his skyrocketing fame redefined what it meant to be a sports star in America.

For the ERNIE NEVERS stamp, Sheaff selected a 1926 photograph from the collection of Stanford University, where Nevers earned an outstanding 11 letters in four sports. Although Stanford lost the 1925 Rose Bowl against Notre Dame and its renowned Four Horsemen, Nevers is nonetheless remembered as the game's hero. Recovering from two broken ankles, he played the game's full 60 minutes while wearing special braces, carrying the ball 34 times, making four out of five tackles, and earning an impressive net gain of 114 yards against the net gain of 126 yards by all Four Horsemen combined. From 1926 to 1927, he played for the Duluth Eskimos, which became known as "Ernie Nevers's Eskimos," and from 1929 to 1931 he played for the Chicago Cardinals. On Thanksgiving Day in 1929, when the Cardinals defeated the Bears with a score of 40 to 6, Nevers scored all 40 points—a one-game professional scoring record that remains the longest-standing record in the NFL.

The stamp honoring BRONISLAU "BRONKO" NAGURSKI, pride of the University of Minnesota Gophers from 1927 to 1929, shows him in his Chicago Bears uniform during a key year in his football career. Nagurski's name was synonymous with the Bears; he played multiple positions for them from 1930 to 1937 and again in 1943. He led them to victory in the first official NFL championship game in 1933, the same year this photo was taken. Nagurski had a reputation for formidable strength, and the photograph on this stamp shows the determined glare that intimidated his fearful opponents. Today he is the inspiration for the Bronko Nagurski Trophy, which is awarded to the defensive college player of the year.

Sheaff is glad that his final designs were able to suggest the strength of these four players and their monumental importance to football.

"I'm quite pleased with the way these stamps have turned out," he says. "These players loved the game and gave it their all. It's only fitting that all these years later, football fans continue to remember the amazing things they did on the field."

FACING PAGE: *In contrast to his fearsome on-field reputation, Bronko Nagurski is remembered as modest and soft-spoken.* TOP: *Bronko Nagurski rushes for a touchdown.* RIGHT: *This piece of college football history commemorates Yale's 1883 victory over Columbia.* LEFT: *A versatile athlete, Ernie Nevers played professional baseball and basketball as well.*

Roy Acuff

WHEN ROY ACUFF BECAME THE FIRST living member of the Country Music Hall of Fame in 1962, the plaque that honored him called him the King of Country Music—an appropriate distinction for the performer whose fame helped turn the Grand Ole Opry into the nation's foremost country music institution.

Born in Maynardville, Tennessee, in 1903, Acuff aspired to be a professional baseball player, but in 1929 a severe case of sunstroke ended his athletic career. While recuperating, he honed his skill with the fiddle, and during the summer of 1932 he performed in a traveling medicine show. He made his first recordings in 1936, and by the end of the decade he and his band, the Smoky

Mountain Boys, had become Grand Ole Opry regulars, due in no small part to a moving performance of a traditional song, "The Great Speckled Bird," that brought Acuff national fame.

For decades, fans loved to hear Acuff perform his renditions of traditional and sacred songs such as "Will the Circle Be Unbroken" and "I Saw the Light," sentimental favorites such as "The Precious Jewel," or songs about trains, especially "Wabash Cannonball." As one of country music's first superstars, Acuff enjoyed a wide-ranging career. He appeared in several movies, ran for governor of Tennessee, performed for American GIs around the world, and co-founded Acuff-Rose Publications, which became the cornerstone of the country-music publishing business.

Faced with more than 50 years of visuals from such a remarkable life, art director Richard Sheaff went back to basics for this stamp, selecting a black-and-white photo taken during the pinnacle of Acuff's career.

Acuff biographer Elizabeth Schlappi researched the photograph for the Postal Service and quickly discovered its source: the March 5, 1949, issue of *Collier's* magazine, where it accompanied an article entitled "Caruso of Mountain Music." The full photo, taken by John E. Hood, also shows Lonnie "Pap" Wilson, a member of Acuff's band, as the two smiling musicians pose with their instruments in front of a mountain cabin.

For Sheaff, this image represents more than just a great vintage country-music scene; the smile on Acuff's face also suggests the joy that he brought to countless fans with the sweet mountain sound of traditional country music.

"In his own way, he was a very colorful character who exuded a certain warmth and sincerity," Sheaff says. "I think this photo reflects that."

ABOVE RIGHT: *The title of one of Acuff's most beloved songs was sometimes spelled in different ways, as shown on this vintage album cover.* ABOVE LEFT: *Another collection of Acuff favorites.* FACING PAGE: *Acuff's vocal style suggested the singing heard in the mountain country churches of his youth.*

Place and Date of Issue	Photographer	Designer and Art Director
Nashville, TN September 13, 2003	**John E. Hood**	**Richard Sheaff**

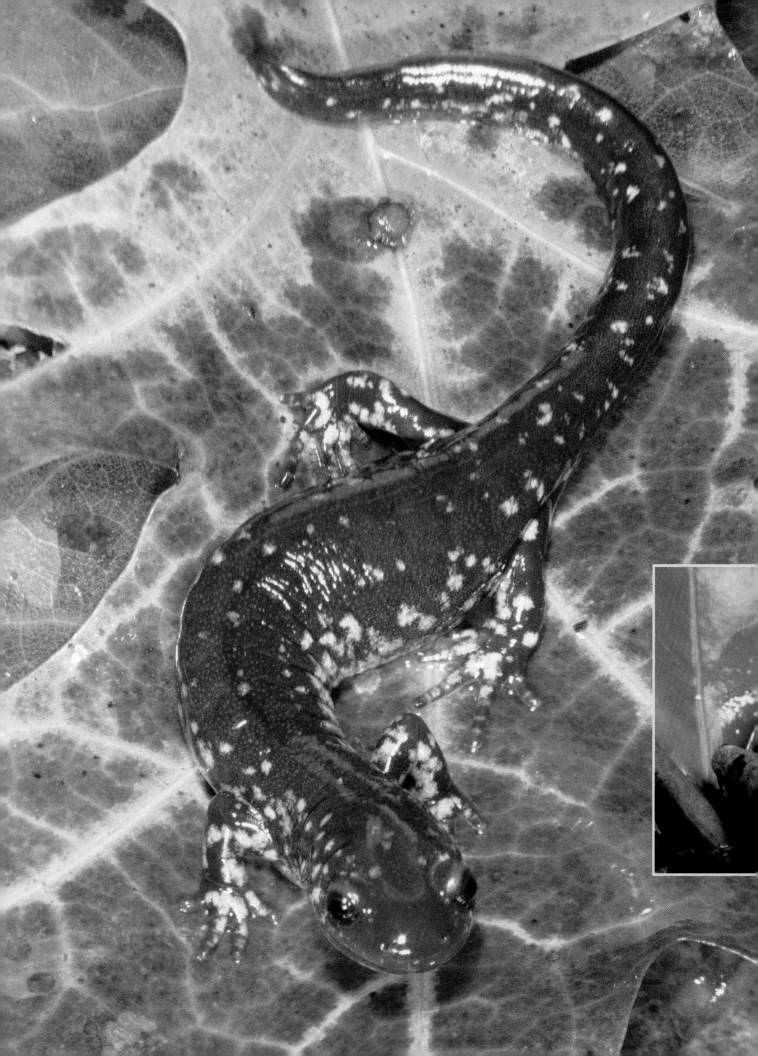

Reptiles and Amphibians

WHEN STEVE BUCHANAN BEGAN the artwork for this year's Reptiles and Amphibians stamps, he gave himself one simple guideline: start with the eyes.

"If a subject has eyes, that's where the viewer's attention is going to be drawn first," says Buchanan, an acclaimed natural science illustrator whose work has appeared in a wide range of books and magazines. "So with these already interesting-looking creatures, I decided to focus on their very intense gaze."

Reptiles and amphibians have long intrigued human observers with their mysterious behavior and beautiful appearances. But when it came time to choose examples to appear on stamps, Buchanan and art director Derry Noyes considered dozens of prospective species before choosing two amphibians and three reptiles that were well suited to be portrayed in such a unique medium.

"Many reptiles and amphibians have colors and patterns that are very ornamental, which is wonderful from a design point of view," says Buchanan. "The challenge is figuring out which of them are likely to look good at stamp size. Some may be beautiful beasts, but they just won't appear distinctive or interesting in a one-inch square."

For Noyes, working with Buchanan on a natural science project is an extremely satisfying experience. "He's just a master at this," she says. "He needs very little art directing, he has a great sense of design, and he really does his homework."

Buchanan's thorough and disciplined approach to his artwork is deeply rooted in his educational background. Trained as a classical musician at Oberlin College in Ohio, he earned his doctorate from the University of Texas at Austin. After eleven years as a music professor and concert pianist, he embarked on his new career—almost entirely by chance.

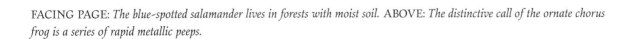

FACING PAGE: *The blue-spotted salamander lives in forests with moist soil.* ABOVE: *The distinctive call of the ornate chorus frog is a series of rapid metallic peeps.*

Place and Date of Issue	Artist and Designer	Art Director
San Diego, CA October 7, 2003	**Steve Buchanan**	**Derry Noyes**

"My wife gave me a copy of the book *Drawing on the Right Side of the Brain*, because she knew that I'd be interested in the author's discussion of different mentalities," Buchanan explains. "Each chapter had exercises, which I completed, and by the time I got to the end of the book I could draw pictures of things."

After studying painting, Buchanan began his remarkable second career as a freelance illustrator in 1988. In addition to his work for the *New York Times*, *Scientific American*, and a host of other prominent publications, Buchanan has also created highly detailed artwork for numerous stamps, including two 1999 issuances, Tropical Flowers and Insects and Spiders, as well as four beguiling Carnivorous Plants stamps in 2001.

"As a hiker and a birdwatcher, I've always been an outdoorsy type, and biology has always interested me," Buchanan says. "In general, I've always been interested in science, whether studying the feathers on a bird or analyzing sound waves using computers."

Buchanan's interest in computers also took him into new creative realms. In particular, his digital illustrations of plants and animals earned him a reputation as an artistic pioneer.

"When I did my first stamps, Tropical Flowers, computer illustration was definitely a novelty," he says. "Now it's pretty mainstream. When I attend the big art and graphic-design shows, more than 20 percent of what I see is created using computers, and I believe that number is rising."

Does technology change the artistic process? Buchanan doesn't think so; on the contrary, he finds that the digital artist still contends with the same challenges and uses many of the same methods.

"It may seem as if working with a computerized drawing pad and using software somehow changes things," he says. "It certainly makes some revisions easier. But we still had to make many of the same design decisions, and the level of research was just as involved. And in the end, the actual experience of being an artist is the same: making marks, darkening shadows, and giving creatures lifelike expressions. That part has hardly changed at all."

LEFT: *The ornate box turtle protects itself by closing its shell completely.* ABOVE RIGHT: *The reticulate-collared lizard may be seen sunning on rocks or found hiding beneath rocks or debris.* FACING PAGE: *The colorful scarlet kingsnake is harmless, but its resemblance to the venomous eastern coral snake protects it from predators.*

Holiday Music Makers

HOLIDAY STAMPS should be joyous reminders of the season, capable of warming the heart even on the coldest of days. That's the effect that Postal Service art director Ethel Kessler had in mind when she happened across a holiday-themed illustration by Diane Teske Harris on the cover of the Weekend section of *The Washington Post*.

"Diane's style was just so delightful," says Kessler. "I had been asked to consider new approaches to lighthearted holiday subjects, and when I saw her warm and colorful technique, I knew she was an artist who would be a wonderful fit for the stamp program."

"Ethel wanted me to work on the theme of a musical Christmas," says Harris, who quickly began developing designs at her studio in Montana. "I sat down and brainstormed and did lots of sketches, including variations on reindeer and Santas playing musical instruments, and we just took it from there."

A prolific commercial artist, Harris has lent her talents to countless magazines, children's textbooks, and even illustrations on candy packaging. With her art in such high demand, she still insists on making every illustration special. In fact, she says that she approaches the drawing board only after placing herself in a calm, meditative mood that helps convey the emotions she hopes to express.

"When I create my work," she says, "I want to convey an upbeat, lighthearted idea of peace and life."

As an artist deeply concerned with spreading positive messages, Harris is enthusiastic about the widespread circulation that stamps enjoy. She takes particular delight in the fact that millions of people will see her festive expressions this year.

"I really like that examples of my artwork will go everywhere, like little emissaries. So if these stamps make just one person smile, that's the sort of thing that really lights my jets."

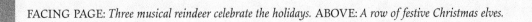

FACING PAGE: *Three musical reindeer celebrate the holidays.* ABOVE: *A row of festive Christmas elves.*

Place and Date of Issue	Artist	Designer and Art Director
New York, NY October 23, 2003	**Diane Teske Harris**	**Ethel Kessler**

61

PHOTO CREDITS

Cover
© Rykoff Collection/CORBIS

Introduction
Page 6
Photo provided by Photofest and used courtesy MGM CLIP+STILL
Page 7
(above left) ©John Springer Collection/CORBIS. *A Streetcar Named Desire* ©1951 Charles Feldman Group Productions
(above right) ©John Springer Collection/CORBIS

Lunar New Year: Year of the Ram
Page 8
(above left) Freer Gallery, Smithsonian Institution, Washington, USA/Bridgeman Art Library
(above right) Stapleton Collection, UK/Bridgeman Art Library
(below right) ©AFP/CORBIS
Page 9
Chester Beatty Library, Dublin/Bridgeman Art Library

Black Heritage: Thurgood Marshall
Page 10
Collection of the Supreme Court of the United States
Page 11
(middle) Courtesy PhotoAssist, Inc., photograph by T. Michael Keza
(right) ©Bettmann/CORBIS

Love
Page 12
(above right) ©Tom Miner/The Image Works
(below left) ©Charles Gatewood /The Image Works

American Filmmaking: Behind the Scenes
Page 14
(above left) *Lawrence of Arabia* ©1962 Horizon Pictures (G.B.) Ltd., renewed 1990 Columbia Pictures Industries, Inc. All rights reserved. Courtesy TriStar Pictures.
(above right) ©Underwood & Underwood/CORBIS
(left) *Postcards from the Edge* ©1990 Columbia Pictures Industries, Inc. All rights reserved. Courtesy TriStar Pictures. Photograph provided by Photofest.
Page 15
(above left) Photograph provided by Photofest
(above right) *E.T. The Extra-Terrestrial* ©1982 Universal City Studios, Inc. Courtesy Universal Studios Licensing LLP.
Page 16
(full page) Ralph Crane/TimePix. Courtesy Paramount Pictures. *The Ten Commandments* ©Paramount Pictures. All rights reserved. Used with permission of the Estate of Cecil B. DeMille.
(inset) *Planet of the Apes* ©1968 Twentieth Century Fox. All rights reserved. Photograph provided by Photofest.
Page 17
(above) ©U.S. Postal Service
(below left) ©U.S. Postal Service, script excerpt courtesy

David O. Selznick Collection, Harry Ransom Humanities Research Center, The University of Texas at Austin
(below right) Ralph Crane/Black Star/TimePix

Ohio Statehood
Page 18
(left) Jeff Greenberg ©The Image Finders
(above right) ©North Wind Picture Archives
(below right) Jim Baron ©The Image Finders
Page 19
(full page) ©2003 Museum of Fine Arts, Boston
(inset) Carl Stimac ©The Image Finders

Pelican Island National Wildlife Refuge
Page 20
(full page) ©Ralph A. Clevenger/CORBIS
(inset) ©Richard Cummins/CORBIS
Page 21
(above left) ©Farrell Grehan/CORBIS
(above right) ©Raymond Gehman/CORBIS

Cesar E. Chavez
Page 22
(left) ©1976 George Ballis/Take Stock
(above) ©1976 George Ballis/Take Stock
Page 23
©1976 Ernest Lowe/Take Stock

Literary Arts: Zora Neale Hurston
Page 24
(full page) ©CORBIS
(signature) Yale Collection of American Literature, Beinecke Rare Book and Manuscript Library
Page 25
(above center) Collection of the Library of Congress, used with permission of HarperCollins Publishers
(above right) Collection of the Library of Congress, used with permission of HarperCollins Publishers
(below left) Yale Collection of American Literature, Beinecke Rare Book and Manuscript Library, used with the permission of the Carl Van Vechten Trust
(below center) Collection of the Library of Congress, used with permission of HarperCollins Publishers

First Flight
Page 26
(above) Courtesy of Special Collections and Archives, Wright State University
(above right) Courtesy of Special Collections and Archives, Wright State University
Page 27
Courtesy of Special Collections and Archives, Wright State University
Page 28
Courtesy of Special Collections and Archives, Wright State University
Page 29
(top) Courtesy of Special Collections and Archives, Wright State University

PHOTO CREDITS

(above) Courtesy of Special Collections and Archives, Wright State University
(below left) Dennis Johnson/FOLIO, Inc.

Louisiana Purchase
Page 30
(above left) ©Royalty-Free/CORBIS
(above right) Courtesy National Archives
Page 31
(far right) National Portrait Gallery, Smithsonian Institution/Art Resource, NY
(left) Courtesy National Archives

American Treasures: Mary Cassatt
Page 32
Musée d'Orsay, Paris, France/Lauros-Giraudon-Bridgeman Art Library
Page 33
(left) F. A. Sweet papers, Archives of American Art, Smithsonian Institution
(right) ©Francis G. Mayer/CORBIS

Southeastern Lighthouses
Page 34
(top left) ©Hib Casselberry
(left) ©Bob Krist/CORBIS
(above right) ©Calvin Larsen/Photo Researchers
Page 35
©Patrik Giardino/CORBIS
Page 36
(full page) ©David Muench/CORBIS
(inset) ©Bob Krist/CORBIS
Page 37
(above) ©Bob Krist/CORBIS
(left) ©Richard Cummins/CORBIS

Korean War Veterans Memorial
Page 38
(above left) ©Wally McNamee/CORBIS
(above right) ©David Douglas Duncan, photograph provided by the Harry Ransom Humanities Research Center, The University of Texas at Austin
Page 39
©Lee Snider/CORBIS

Old Glory
Page 40
Courtesy Timothy Shaner
Page 41
(above right) ©David Pollack/CORBIS
(middle left) ©Charles Traub/Woodfin Camp
(right) ©Lake County Museum/CORBIS
Page 42
(above) ©Lake County Museum/CORBIS
(left) ©Lake County Museum/CORBIS
(right) Collection of the American Folk Art Museum, New York
Page 43
©Owen Franken/CORBIS

Nature of America: Arctic Tundra
Page 44
©Scott T. Smith/CORBIS
Page 45
(above right) ©Pat O'Hara/CORBIS
(above left) ©Scott T. Smith/CORBIS
(right) ©2003 Johnny Johnson/AlaskaStock.com

District of Columbia
Page 46
(above left) ©Catherine Karnow/CORBIS
(above right) ©CORBIS
(lower right) ©Catherine Karnow/CORBIS
Page 47
©H. David Seawell/CORBIS

Legends of Hollywood: Audrey Hepburn
Page 48
MPTV.net. Courtesy of Paramount Pictures. *Breakfast at Tiffany's* ©Paramount Pictures. All rights reserved.
Page 49
(above) Bob Willoughby/MPTV.net
(left) Unicef/HQ90-0081/Peter Charlesworth

Early Football Heroes
Page 50
(above left) ©Bettmann/CORBIS
(above right) Photograph by Mark Jones, University of Illinois Sports Information
(right) ©Bettmann/CORBIS
Page 51
Courtesy Yale Athletic Department Archives
Page 52
Getty Images/Hulton Archive
Page 53
(top) ©CORBIS
(right) Courtesy Yale Athletic Department Archives
(left) Everett Collection/CSU

Roy Acuff
Page 54
(above right) Courtesy Columbia Records
(above left) Courtesy Capitol Records
Page 55
Courtesy Country Music Association

Reptiles and Amphibians
Page 56
©John M. Burnley/Photo Researchers, Inc.
Page 57
©Jack Dermid/Photo Researchers, Inc.
Page 58
(left) Zig Leszczynski/Animals Animals
(above right) ©David T. Roberts/Photo Researchers, Inc.
Page 59
©Charles Philip/CORBIS

Holiday Music Makers
Pages 60–61
©2003 Diane Teske Harris

ACKNOWLEDGMENTS

These stamps and this stamp-collecting book were produced by Stamp Services, Government Relations, United States Postal Service.

JOHN E. POTTER
Postmaster General,
Chief Executive Officer

RALPH J. MODEN
Senior Vice President,
Government Relations and Public Policy

DAVID E. FAILOR
Executive Director,
Stamp Services

Special thanks are extended to the following individuals for their contributions to the production of this book:

UNITED STATES POSTAL SERVICE

TERRENCE W. MCCAFFREY
Manager, Stamp Development

SONJA D. EDISON
Project Manager

HARPERCOLLINS PUBLISHERS

MEGAN NEWMAN
Editorial Director,
HarperResource

NICK DARRELL
Assistant Editor,
HarperResource

LUCY ALBANESE
Design Director,
General Books Group

NIGHT & DAY DESIGN

TIMOTHY SHANER
Art Director, Designer

PHOTOASSIST, INC.

JEFF SYPECK
Copywriter

GREG VARNER
Text Research

MIKE OWENS
Photo Editor
Rights and Permissions

THE CITIZENS' STAMP ADVISORY COMMITTEE

DR. VIRGINIA M. NOELKE
CARY R. BRICK
MICHAEL R. BROCK
MEREDITH J. DAVIS
DAVID L. EYNON
JEAN PICKER FIRSTENBERG
SYLVIA HARRIS
I. MICHAEL HEYMAN
JOHN M. HOTCHNER
DR. C. DOUGLAS LEWIS
KARL MALDEN
RICHARD F. PHELPS
RONALD A. ROBINSON
JOHN SAWYER III